Butterfly Notes

Story by
Dianne Wolfer

Illustrated by
Diana Platt

Rigby PM Plus Chapter Books
part of the Rigby PM Program
Emerald Level

U.S. edition © 2003 Rigby Education
A division of Reed Elsevier Inc.
1000 Hart Road
Barrington, IL 60010 - 2627
www.rigby.com

Text © 2003 Dianne Wolfer
Illustrations © 2003 Thomson Learning Australia
Originally published in Australia by Thomson Learning Australia

10 9 8 7 6 5 4 3 2
07 06 05 04

Butterfly Notes
    ISBN 0 7578 4121 X

Printed in China by Midas Printing (Asia) Ltd

Contents

Chapter One

Five Days to Go

Only five days until I play my violin in the school concert. Help!

I'll have to walk onto the stage at school. Just me – Sarah Wood and my violin. It gives me butterflies thinking about it. Last year I performed with the other kids in Mrs. Rondo's violin group. That was pretty scary, even though there were twelve of us. This year I'm doing a solo and I'm terrified!

After the solo, I'm in a duet with my friend, Stefan. He's really good, so I'm not too nervous about that. Then we'll also play four songs with the rest of our violin group. That should be okay because if you make a mistake, the others drown you out. It's the solo I'm worried about!

Mom says to ignore the butterflies and they'll go away, but I like Grandma's idea for dealing with them.

Grandma says that when the butterflies begin fluttering around my tummy, I should welcome them! Getting butterflies means that a chemical called adrenalin is charging through my blood and will make me play better. This sounds very weird to me, but Grandma was a doctor before she retired, so I guess she knows.

And there's more...

After welcoming the butterflies, Grandma suggests focusing on them.

"Let them fly from your tummy into your chest," she says. "Let them collect passion from your heart to take along your arm into your bow. Then imagine the butterflies changing into musical notes. Let them soar from your violin, off the stage, and into the audience."

Yeah, sure! Grandma tends to be dramatic. She acts in the community theater group. I like her butterfly idea – really! It's just that when I get nervous, I can't think straight, so how can I imagine a butterfly migration?

Maybe Mom's advice is best after all. I cross another day off the calendar. Tomorrow it will be only...

Chapter Two

Four Days to Go

Tomorrow is my last lesson before the concert. Mrs. Rondo gave me a list of things to practice. It's almost a mile long! Stefan's coming over today. We need to practice our duet. The doorbell rings. I bet it's him...

"Hi Stefan," I say.

"How's it going?" he smiles.

"Slowly! I'm not sure if I'm counting the beats properly."

"Let's put on the CD and see."

Stefan is only three months older than me, but he is much calmer. He's also really talented. There's something special about the way he plays his violin. It's as if he *feels* the music flowing from somewhere deep inside. I asked him about it once, but he blushed and changed the subject. He's very modest! We've been friends since preschool. I'm lucky to have him as my duet partner.

Stefan's family lives on the farm next door. I guess that's why Mrs. Rondo suggested we perform together. It would have been hard to practice a duet with a kid from town. Stefan is way ahead of me in lessons. Sometimes I worry about that, and wonder if Stefan minds playing a piece that is so easy for him.

Stefan puts on the CD and we begin. He plays the harmony while I play the melody.

Stefan and I are like two threads running through the same piece of music. Sometimes it's his turn to be loud, and then it's mine. He nods to me as he finishes each bar.

Then it's time to practice *without* the CD. We take our violins out to the shed. It has good acoustics, and there's a bench we use as our stage.

I pretend not to see my annoying twin brothers spying on us.

"Ready?" Stefan asks. The butterflies surge, but I nod.

We bow and imagine applause from the audience. Then Stefan counts us in.

"One, two, three, four…"

The butterflies start dive-bombing. They tickle my belly and I mess up the entry. Stefan must hate playing with me!

Stefan smiles and tells me it's okay. He knows about my butterflies. I try to ignore those pesky insects, but they won't leave! Stefan counts us in and we're away. Hooray!

"Isn't this a beautiful tune?" Stefan says as we finish. "I love playing it."

I smile. That's one less thing to worry about!

We play it again and then once more to be sure.

"Race you back," Stefan says.

"Don't run with your violins!" Mom shrieks as we cross the yard. She has a snack waiting in the kitchen. Banana cake – my favorite. As we lick the frosting, I cross off another day.

Chapter Three

Three Days to Go

Today the violin group is practicing on the school stage! I try not to look at the rows of empty seats.

"How are the butterflies going?" Mom asks. She's waiting to drive Stefan and me back home, after practice.

"Fine," I fib.

"That's good," she says. "Well, I'll just pop out and do some shopping until the end of your lesson. Is that okay?"

I nod. Mom loves coming into town.

"Okay, everyone," Mrs. Rondo calls, "let's practice the group medley first."

We tune up and launch into the medley. It's easy and I love playing it. Mrs. Rondo tells us we sound like one violin. That's her ultimate compliment! Then we play another song in a round of three. It's hard for the younger kids to get the timing, so we do it again and again. Stefan and I roll our eyes. Mrs. Rondo notices and scolds us. At last they get it right, and we finish with a catchy tune. I can't help tapping my toes.

Finally we take turns playing our solos. The butterflies have a party in my stomach, and I have to stop halfway.

"Don't worry, Sarah," Mrs. Rondo says. "It's just nerves. You'll be fine on the day." I nod miserably. Maybe!

Back home, I feed the chickens and do my homework. As I put my school books away, I notice that I've doodled butterflies all down the margins of my page. Aargh! I cross off another day and get ready for bed.

Chapter Four

Two Days to Go

Grandma and Pop are coming for dinner.

"Pop can't come to the concert, but he wants to hear your solo," Mom says.

Mom is cooking roast lamb and Dad has promised to make his special lemon pudding, but I've lost my appetite. Can't we forget about my solo for a while? At least until after dinner! Mom gives me "that look."

Everyone sits in the living room and I have to pretend to come on from backstage. As I bow, the twins make rude noises. Mom sends them out of the room.

"One, two, three," says Pop.

I lift my bow. The beginning is fine. Then I imagine a crowd of faces staring at me. Butterflies zoom in all directions. I drop my bow and run from the room. Grandma follows. I try to hide my tears, but she sees them.

"Why can't I be like Stefan?" I ask her. "He makes it look so easy."

"We can't all be alike, but never mind," Grandma replies. "You're determined, like me – it may take longer, but you'll get there in the end. Now dry your eyes! We need to sort out those butterflies of yours."

I sniff and she pulls out a pink handkerchief from her pocket. It smells just like Grandma.

"Okay, take a deep breath! Now, start playing your solo and imagine yourself on stage," Grandma says. "That's it, keep playing. Now, everyone is watching you. Are the butterflies flapping?"

I nod.

"What color are they?"

"Blue. Like big Ulysses butterflies."

"Right," says Grandma. "When you get to the part where you have to play quickly, imagine a mob of those blue butterflies flying into your chest. Let the audience hear their beating wings. Then, during the quieter part that follows, let them flit along your arm, ready to fly forth in a big splash at the end."

"Won't it be worse if I think about them?"

"I don't think so. They're already in your tummy. You may as well use their energy. What do you think?"

I shrug my shoulders.

"Come on! Let's give it a try."

"Okay," I mumble.

Grandma puts her arm around my shoulders, and we go into the kitchen. Nobody mentions the concert during dinner, not even my brothers! After a second helping of Dad's lemon pudding, I cross off another day.

Chapter Five

One Day to Go

After school, I take my violin into the shed. My brothers begin circling, but I'm not in the mood for games.

"Get lost," I tell them fiercely and, to my surprise, they scatter.

Dragon and Fly, our dogs, follow me into the shed. They like listening to me play, unlike the sheep which panic as soon as my bow touches the strings. Dad says not to worry, sheep aren't very musical!

As I play, I think about all the things that could go wrong.

1.   I could drop my bow.

2.   I could forget my piece.

3.   I could miss a note.

4.   I could burst into tears...

Yikes! Why did I agree to this? The butterflies gather into clusters in my stomach and begin flapping.

"Stop it!" I shout. Dragon and Fly look up, surprised, and I wonder if they can hear the wings zooming around my stomach. I must control them! But how?

I remember Dad spent ages training the dogs. When I helped, he told me I was a natural. Surely butterflies can't be that much harder! I put down my violin and begin giving orders. I wish I could just cross them all out – like I cross out the days on the calendar.

Chapter Six

Today!

At last the day of the concert is here. I'm relieved *and* panic-stricken! Can you be both at the same time?

We pick up Stefan and drive to town. Stefan and I go backstage to tune up. There is a mirror in the practice room and I look at my reflection. Mom has tied my hair into a knot and lots of blue butterfly clips float across my head – presents from Grandma!

I stare at the clips and remember Grandma's words, "Use their energy."

On stage, the announcer tells a bad joke.

"And here's a musical one... What do you get when you cross a mummy with a CD player?" No one answers. "Wrap music!"

Oh no. Even my jokes are better than that. The audience laughs politely. Then he continues.

"And now, let's continue with the Under 13 strings, here's performer number three..."

I walk on stage and bow. Everyone claps and I freeze. A mass of brilliant blue butterflies whiz around my tummy. Time stops as I stare at the crowd, gulping like a goldfish. Someone coughs and then I see Grandma. Her mouth is moving. "Use their energy..."

I lift my violin and the audience relaxes. The butterflies dive-bomb my belly as I begin to play. I close my eyes as I reach the fast part; then as my bow flies over the strings, I herd the butterflies into my chest. My playing becomes louder, then softens as the butterflies flit along my arms. Not long to go... I open my eyes as the butterflies fly from my violin strings and soar into the audience. It's over. I didn't drop my bow, or miss a note, or cry. In fact, I think I played well!

Mom and Dad and Grandma are grinning. Even my annoying brothers are clapping wildly and yelling, "Whoo-hoo!" I bow to the audience and walk off stage.

"Well done!" Stefan whispers.

It's his turn next. "Good luck," I reply, grinning.

As Stefan walks out, I peek from behind the curtain. Grandma is wiping her eyes with her pink handkerchief. Is it my imagination, or can I see a flock of beautiful butterflies hovering over her?

I hold my breath and concentrate on my stomach. The butterflies are gone! Grandma's trick worked! I smile. My Grandma is amazing. I watch Stefan bowing. It's not long until our duet, and now that I have learned to master my butterflies, I can't wait to go back on stage!